YEMEN

Customs & Cultural Heritage

A Guide to the Customs and
Culture of Yemen.

By Tariq Al-Khalil

Table of Contents

Introduction

I. Yemeni Culture

With a long past and important roots in Arab and Islamic customs, Yemeni culture is rich and varied. Yemeni society is focused on family and community, and social relationships are built on strong bonds of relatives and shared ideas.

Visitors are frequently greeted with wide arms and given incredibly nice treatment because kindness, charity, and respect for elders are highly prized.

The majority of the people in Yemen are Muslim, and the country has a highly religious society. Every part of Yemeni culture is infused with Islamic principles and customs, from daily prayer and Ramadan fasting to traditional clothes and food.

Yemeni culture, however, is highly varied, with clear regional differences and impacts from nearby nations and cultures.

Yemeni food boasts a wide range of tastes and products, making it a part of the nation's culture. Yemeni food is known for its use of herbs and spices including cumin, coriander, turmeric, and saffron, and is frequently spicy and aromatic.

Mandi (slow-cooked meat and rice), Salta (spicy stew with veggies and meat), and Aseedah are some of the most well-known Yemeni recipes (porridge made from ground wheat and meat).

Yemeni society also puts a strong focus on writing and art, with a long past of poems, music, and dance.

Yemen music, which combines both classical and local styles, is marked by the use of native instruments such as the oud (a sort of lute) and the mizmar (a type of flute). Yemeni literature is likewise vast and varied, having a long history of religious studies, poetry, and storytelling.

Yemeni culture is nevertheless strong and stubborn, with a strong feeling of community and a high regard for custom and memory, despite the country's many problems.

II. The Value of Knowing Yemeni Culture

It's crucial to understand Yemeni society for a variety of reasons.

Fostering Cultural Understanding: People from other countries can better understand the unique habits, values, and customs of the Yemeni people by learning about Yemeni culture. Building links between different countries and encouraging cross-cultural knowledge and respect can both gain from this.

Enabling Trade and Business: Yemen is a major player in the global economy, and knowledge of its culture can help both people and businesses in managing the nation's economic practices and customs. This can make business links easy and support investment and trade.

Developing Better International Relationships: Yemen is an important Muslim-majority country in the Middle East. Knowing its culture can promote stronger ties between Yemen and other countries and encourage more cooperation on topics of shared interest.

Promoting Peace and Stability: Understanding Yemen's culture can help to create more understanding and respect amongst different groups and support efforts to promote peace and stability in the nation. Yemen has recently faced serious political and social unrest.

Improving Personal Enrichment: Lastly, learning about Yemeni culture can improve personal enrichment by giving insights into other lives and views on the world. One's outlook may change as a result, and one may develop a greater respect for the range and depth of human experience.

Avoid Cultural Misunderstanding: To avoid accidental insult or rudeness, for instance, it can be helpful to know how to meet someone politely, what motions to avoid, and what talking topics to stay clear of.

Maintaining Cultural Heritage: Yemen has a rich cultural past that includes historic buildings, regional crafts, and an original branch of Islamic study. It is possible to support the protection of this past and stop it from being lost or forgotten by knowing Yemeni culture.

Promoting Human Rights: Knowing Yemeni culture may also help in the promotion of human rights and the protection of the abuse of cultural rights. For instance, knowing Yemen customs and practices can help to stop the abuse or exploitation of women, children, and disadvantaged groups.

Enabling Humanitarian Aid: Millions of people in Yemen are currently in need of food, water, and medical care due to a humanitarian disaster. Humanitarian aid workers can better serve people in need by giving thoughtful and appropriate assistance by having a full understanding of Yemeni society.

Improving Global Citizenship: Gaining a better understanding of Yemeni culture can make people better global citizens who value the range of human experience as well as international communication and teamwork. This might lead to a world that is more quiet and peaceful.

III. Geography of Yemen

The Arabian Peninsula's southwest area is where Yemen is located. Its northern limit is with Saudi Arabia, its eastern border with Oman, its western border with the Red Sea, and its southern border with the Gulf of Aden and the Arabian Sea.

Rugged mountains, green rivers, and huge deserts make up the nation's varied scenery. Many important rivers, including the Bab el-Mandeb Strait that connects the Red Sea to the Gulf of Aden, are also found in Yemen.

Yemen's past is vast and diverse, spanning thousands of years. Ancient Yemen was a prominent center of society, with the towns of Sana'a, Marib, and Aden acting as important hubs of trade and culture.

Yemen was a major center of Islamic study and learning and was vital to the Arabian Peninsula's turn to Islam.

Yemen has been ruled by several powers and families throughout its history, including the Sabean Kingdom, the Himyarite Kingdom, the Islamic Caliphate, the Zaydi Imams, and the Ottoman Empire.

North Yemen and South Yemen were the two separate states that made up Yemen in the 20th century.

Although the two countries were unified in 1990, there have been many political and economic problems since then.

Yemen has had a terrible civil war in recent years that has led to a great deal of suffering and homeless people.

Many factors, like political and economic complaints, rivalry on the regional and international levels, and ethnic tensions, have added to the war.

Despite these difficulties, Yemen continues to have a lively culture and a strong people that is working to fix the nation and move it toward a more peaceful and prosperous future.

CHAPTER I

Yemeni Society & Values

1.1 Family and Community Structures

Yemeni society is focused on family and community, and close ties among cousins and a set of shared ideals affect how people connect.

The family is seen as the basis of society, and Yemeni homes are often big and extended, with many generations living in the same home.

The oldest male family member often acts as the head of the home in Yemeni society, which is patriarchal. Nonetheless, women have a major part in the family and are often in charge of running the home and rearing the kids.

Younger family members are supposed to respect and obey their adults, and respect for parents is highly prized.

In Yemen, group organizations are likewise built on strong ties to one another and a shared set of ideals. Yemeni groups are often small and have a strong feeling of duty and dedication to one another.

People often turn to their friends and extended families for help and support, especially during tough times.

Yemeni social and religious practices also show a feeling of togetherness. For instance, smoking qat, a mild narcotic plant that is popular in Yemen is a tradition that is often shared with friends and family.

Similar to this, religious holidays and events often serve as chances for neighborhood get-togethers and social links.

In general, Yemeni family and community organizations are defined by a strong feeling of connection and duty, as well as by a deep regard for history and shared ideals.

1.2 Relationships & Gender Roles

Traditional Islamic culture, which strongly values humility and respect for gender-specific duties, has a deep effect on gender roles and interactions in Yemen.

The standard gender positions of males as the major breadwinners and women as the home managers and kid providers are usually expected of men and women.

In Yemen, women may have limits on their freedom of movement and social contacts, as well as limited access to schooling and work opportunities. Strong cultural practices that stress the importance of women's duties in the family and society exist as well, however.

Yemeni society, especially for women, strongly values humility and purity in human relations.

In Yemen, planned weddings are widespread while dating is rare. Families often play a key part in the selection of a suitable mate since marriage is considered a social and religious duty.

Nonetheless, other traditional practices stress the value of support and love for one another in marriage. For instance, the idea of mahr, a monetary gift that must be given by the groom to the bride at the time of the wedding, aims to provide the wife with financial safety and support the concept of teamwork within the marriage.

Generally, Yemen's gender roles and relationships are difficult and diverse, representing a mix of traditional Islamic culture, social facts, and changing ideas regarding gender and family interactions.

1.3 Generosity and Hospitality

In Yemeni culture, kindness and politeness are also highly valued traits. Yemenis are famous for their hospitality and open-arms approach to guests.

Strangers are often welcomed into Yemeni homes for tea or coffee, and Yemenis take great joy in making their tourists feel welcome.

Even though they are strangers, it is seen as a duty in the Yemeni culture to feed and house guests.

This custom, called "diyyafah," has a long past in Yemeni society. Yemenis will go above and above to make sure that their guests are at ease and well-cared for.

Yemeni society puts a high value on charity. Yemenis are driven to give back to their neighborhoods and help those in need. Yemenis often give presents to others, especially during religious holidays and other important events.

Yemeni food shows the country's friendliness and kindness. In Yemen, meals are often shared with family and friends, and guests are frequently welcome to join. Yemeni food is famous for its strong taste and big serving sizes.

In summary, Yemeni society puts a high value on giving and kindness.

Yemenis take great pleasure in providing their guests with a nice time and are well-recognized for their polite hospitality and warm welcome.

Yemenis place a high value on kindness and helping people in need as well as giving back to their local areas.

1.4 The Value of Honesty and Shame

In Yemeni culture, respect and shame are strongly established and have a big effect on how people act and behave. In Yemen, the idea of "Sharaf," which is highly regarded, sits at the heart of the concept of honor.

Sharaf is gained via one's actions and behaviors and is linked to honor, respect, and image.

Honor is directly linked to family and group identity in Yemeni society. The actions of one person affect the image of their whole family and the neighborhood.

As a result, Yemeni families put a high value on keeping their respect and refraining from any actions that can make them seem bad.

Shame is often linked in Yemeni society to actions that are seen as evil or unethical, such as lying, deceiving, or showing contempt. Shame may also be linked to financial difficulties or the inability to support one's family.

Serious consequences, such as social rejection and loss of respect, may result from actions that bring one's family or oneself into disrepute.

The ritual of taking revenge, called "tha'r," is another example of how important honor and shame are. In Yemeni society, it is one's duty to seek revenge to restore one's respect if one's honor or the honor of one's family is harmed.

Tha'r is seen as an important measure to protect one's honor and secure one's image, and it may include a circle of violence that lasts for generations.

In conclusion, Yemeni culture puts a high value on respect and shame. Yemeni families put a high value on keeping their respect and avoiding any actions that can reflect badly on them.

Serious consequences, such as social rejection and loss of respect, may result from actions that bring one's family or oneself into disrepute. The idea of honor is strongly linked to family and clan identity, and getting even is seen to be the only way to keep one's honor and protect one's image.

CHAPTER II

Religion in Yemen

2.1 Overview of Islam in Yemen

With more than 99% of the people reporting as Muslim, Islam is the main faith in Yemen.

While a large group of Zaydi Shia Muslims live in Yemen, Sunni Muslims make up the bulk of the people. Yemen is well known for its strong dedication to Islamic beliefs and values, which are rooted in Yemeni culture and practices.

In Yemen, social fairness and a strong feeling of community are important to the religion of Islam. The Friday prayers are a very important part of the holy week for Yemeni Muslims, who put considerable importance on praying and going to churches.

Islamic beliefs place a high value on kindness, ethics, and respect for others, and many parts of everyday life display these qualities.

Another important part of Yemeni religious life is the Islamic calendar. Islam-related holidays including Ramadan, Eid al-Fitr, and Eid al-Adha are held nationally. Muslims fast from dawn till dusk throughout Ramadan, which is a time for thought and greater dedication.

The Grand Mosque of Sana'a, one of the largest mosques in the world, is only one of the important Islamic buildings that can be found in Yemen.

In addition, the nation has a long past of Islamic art and building, which is evident in the many churches, tombs, and other structures that dot the landscape.

Yemen has always been a major hub for Islamic education and learning, and its past is closely linked with the history of Islam.

Yemen has produced several well-known Islamic teachers and leaders, including Imam al-Bukhari, who is well-known for collecting hadiths, or sayings of the Prophet Muhammad.

Yemeni society and habits have a strong Islamic impact. Muslims in Yemen put a high importance on praying, going to churches, and sticking to Islamic rules and customs.

Yemeni Muslims have long made large contributions to Islamic study and learning. The country has a rich Islamic heritage, with numerous notable Islamic sites and landmarks.

2.2 Religious Customs & Rituals

Yemen is a largely Muslim country, and Islamic beliefs and practices are deeply rooted in day-to-day life.

Some of the Islamic customs and rites followed by Yemeni Muslims are the ones mentioned below:

Prayer: Five times a day, Yemeni Muslims offer prayers while facing the Kaaba in Mecca, which is said to be the greatest place in Islam.

Fasting: Muslims in Yemen fast from sunrise to dusk during the holy month of Ramadan. Spiritual reflection and greater loyalty to God are fitting at this time.

Zakat: In Yemen, Muslims are required to give a certain portion of their money to a charity, called zakat. One of Islam's five pillars is seen as a method to cleanse one's wealth and help those in need.

Hajj: The Hajj, or journey to the greatest place in Islam, draws millions of Muslims from all over the world to Mecca each year. If they can, Yemeni Muslims also take part in this trip.

Al-Fitr and Eid Al-Adha: The two most important Islamic holidays, Eid al-Fitr and Eid al-Adha are held in Yemen. Ramadan comes to a close with Eid al-Fitr, and Eid al-Adha celebrates Abraham for giving up his son as a gift to God.

Friday Prayers: Muslims in Yemen visit the mosque for the Friday noon prayer, which is highly important in Islam. This is a chance for the community to come together and listen to the imam's speech.

Religious Education: The study of Islam is highly valued in Yemen, where many Muslims go to madrassas, or Islamic schools, to learn more about the religion and to read the Quran.

Quran Recitation: Reading and reading the Quran is very important to Yemeni Muslims since it is the holy book of Islam. The whole Quran is learned by many Yemeni Muslims, and reading it is seen as an act of piety.

Dhikr: Dhikr is a way of remembering God that involves repeating certain words or prayers. Yemeni Muslims do dhikr to improve their spiritual ties to God.

Pilgrimages to Religious Places: The Grand Mosque of Sana'a and the Shrine of Imam Ali in Aden are two of Yemen's numerous important Islamic structures and sites. Yemeni Muslims often visit these places as pilgrimages to improve their religion and connect with their spiritual roots.

Family and Community Meetings: These are held in homes and churches in Yemen, where Muslims put a high value on these ideas. These meetings provide people a chance to join for prayer, Quran reading, and meals.

Modesty: Islamic society places a high value on modesty, and Yemeni Muslims often dress carefully with women covering their heads and wearing loose-fitting clothes.

Personal Hygiene: Muslims in Yemen often do ablutions, or ritual baths, before prayer since it is thought that personal cleanliness is a crucial component of Islamic practice.

Commitment to Islamic Law: Sharia, or Islamic law, is a major part of Yemeni society and is used in many aspects of everyday life, such as business deals, property, and marriage.

In conclusion, Yemeni Muslims follow a wide range of religious customs and practices, such as reading the Qur'an, doing the dhikr, going on pilgrimages, spending time with family and friends, dressing modestly, keeping good personal health, and living by Islamic law.

These practices are seen as a means of improving one's religion and creating ties with the bigger Islamic society.

2.3 Religion's Role in Everyday Life

In Yemen, many people's everyday lives are highly affected by their faith views. Yemeni culture and society are highly affected by Islam in particular, and this can be noticed in many parts of everyday life.

Following are a few examples of how religion influences Yemeni everyday life:

Prayer: Five times a day, Muslims in Yemen offer prayers, which are often preceded by the call to prayer, which is heard across the towns and cities. One way to connect with God and ask for His instructions and forgiveness is via prayer.

Fasting: Muslims in Yemen fast from sunrise to dusk during the holy month of Ramadan. This means denying oneself food, drink, and other physical pleasures. Fasting is seen as a method to improve one's devotion to God and cleanse the heart.

Charity: Muslims in Yemen are required to provide Zakat, or a portion of their wealth, to charity. This is seen as a means to cleanse one's wealth and help those who are in need.

Religious Instruction: The study of Islam is highly valued in Yemen, where a large number of kids attend madrassas, or Islamic schools, to learn about Islam and the Quran. faith education is seen as a way of growing one's faith beliefs and understanding of Islam.

Family: In Yemeni culture, the family is valued highly, and many facets of family life are affected by religion. For instance, according to Islamic law, divorce is only authorized in certain situations and marriage is seen as a sacred commitment.

Business Customs: Sharia, or Islamic law, is used in many facets of Yemeni trade and business. This comprises regulations governing contracts, disputes, and interests.

Social Interactions: Islamic traditions and practices have a significant effect on many social interactions in Yemen. For instance, welcomes often entail the exchanging of religious idioms, and Ramadan sees a large gathering of Yemeni families to break the fast.

In conclusion, many individuals in Yemen's everyday lives are significantly influenced by religion, especially Islam. It affects a wide range of facets of life, including social relations, education, family life, business operations, and fasting and prayer.

CHAPTER III

Yemeni Language & Communication

3.1 Introduction to Yemeni Arabic

Yemenis generally converse with one another in Yemeni Arabic, which is the country's official language.

An Arabic dialect spoken in Yemen is called Yemeni Arabic. It is a variety of Arabic that has been molded by the specific historical and cultural background of the region.

The following are some fundamental aspects of Yemeni Arabic:

Pronunciation: Yemeni Arabic has a distinctive pronunciation that distinguishes it different from other dialects of the language. For instance, the letter "qaf" contains a glottal stop whereas the word "jim" frequently sounds like the letter "sh."

Vocabulary: It's a good idea to have a backup plan in place, particularly if you're going to be traveling a lot. More words were borrowed from other languages, including Turkish, Persian, and English.

Grammar: Yemeni Arabic has a similar fundamental grammar to other Arabic dialects, but, there are noteworthy variations in the way verbs are conjugated and nouns are declined.

Dialect: Yemeni Arabic has various dialects, each of which differs according to the area and the local cultural influences. The most frequently used dialects of Arabic are Ta'izzi-Adeni, Hadhrami, and Sana'ani.

Tribal Culture Influence: Tribal cultures that have historically existed in the region have affected Yemeni Arabic. Because of this, the vocabulary and pronunciation differ depending on the tribe or area.

Media Use: Yemeni Arabic is extensively used in newspapers, magazines, radio programs, and television broadcasts. Social media and other online platforms also regularly employ it.

Daily Use: Yemeni Arabic is the major language used for communication between friends and family members and is actively employed in daily life in Yemen. Moreover, it is a common language of instruction in many schools and is employed in commerce and trade.

Influence of Islam: Islam's imprint may also be noticed in Yemeni Arabic as Islam is the country's official religion. This may be noticed in ordinary speech and phrases as well as in the employment of religious terminology and salutations.

Hospitality: Hospitality is revered highly in Yemeni culture, which is also represented in Yemeni Arabic. Ahlan wa sahlan, which means "welcome," and "ma'alesh," which means "never mind" or "no issue," are just a few of the various words and concepts that have to do with hospitality.

Poetry and Literature: Yemeni Arabic has a strong tradition of poetry and literature, and it has produced many well-known poets and novelists over the years. Yemeni culture considers poetry as a prominent art form, and it is widely recited at social gatherings and other events.

Effect of other Languages: Turkish, Persian, and English have all had an effect on Yemeni Arabic over time. The employment of phrases and idioms that have been adopted from many languages demonstrates this.

Regional Variations: Yemeni Arabic is spoken all over Yemen, but there are regional variants in vocabulary, pronunciation, and grammar. The particular cultural and historical context of the location typically influences these differences.

Yemeni Arabic plays a key significance in the country's culture and way of life. It has been impacted by the region's specific historical and cultural heritage, as well as by Islam and other languages.

Yemeni Arabic has a lengthy history of poetry and literature and is frequently employed in daily life. The language's regional varieties reflect the richness of Yemeni culture and history.

3.2 Linguistic Dialects and Varieties

Yemeni Arabic comprises various dialects that change according to location and local cultural factors.

A handful of the dialects that are most regularly utilized include:

Sana'ani Arabic: The capital city of Sana'a and its surrounds are home to speakers of the Sana'ani dialect of Arabic. It is recognized as one of the most known dialects in Yemen and is differentiated by its peculiar pronunciation and vocabulary.

Hadhrami Arabic: The Hadhramaut region in southern Yemen is home to the Hadhrami Arabic dialect, which is characterized by its distinctive lexicon and sound. It has been strongly impacted by the region's long-standing linkages to East Africa and India.

Ta'iz-Adeni Arabic: This dialect, which is used in Ta'iz and Aden, is differentiated by its peculiar pronunciation and vocabulary. The old trade routes that flowed through the region have had an influence.

Yemeni Bedouin Arabic: Arabic spoken by the Bedouin tribes of Yemen is known as Yemeni Bedouin Arabic and is distinguishable by its distinct vocabulary and tone. Tribal cultures that have historically existed in the region have impacted it.

Dialects vary widely from place to location and each has its particular traits.

Despite these variances, all Yemeni Arabic dialects maintain a similar vocabulary and grammatical structure that allow speakers from diverse areas to converse.

3.3 Nonverbal Communication

Similar to many other civilizations, Yemeni culture puts a great priority on nonverbal communication.

Key characteristics of nonverbal communication in Yemen include the following:

Eye Contact: In Yemeni culture, establishing direct eye contact with someone who has a higher social standing is viewed as a display of respect. Direct eye contact between folks of different genders isn't always ideal, though.

Facial Expression: Yemenis typically send messages and feelings via their facial expressions. For instance, a smile may suggest delight or camaraderie, yet a scowl might imply anger or disapproval.

Gestures: Gestures are also frequently utilized in Yemeni communication. A sign of agreement or understanding, for instance, might be a nod of the head, whereas an indicator of disagreement or confusion may be a shake of the head.

Postures: In Yemeni culture, posture may also have a symbolic value. Slouching or crossing one's arms could be viewed as an indicator of disdain or defensiveness whereas sitting with an open, relaxed posture is considered as a statement of confidence and respect.

Touch: In Yemeni culture, touch is a less prominent way of nonverbal communication, particularly between persons of different genders. Physical contact, such as hugging or patting on the back, is prevalent and acceptable as a symbol of affection when it happens between family members or close friends.

Silence: In Yemeni culture, silence may be a major sort of nonverbal communication.

Pauses are commonly used to indicate respect or pondering in speaking. Silence may also be used to signify discomfort or discontent.

Dress: In Yemeni culture, dress and garments may also communicate importance. The abaya and hijab worn by women and the thobe and shawl worn by males are believed to be markers of respect and cultural identity. Clothing may also communicate social position or a person's religious views.

Handshakes: In Yemeni culture, greeting one another with a handshake is common. To follow the example of the person you are meeting, it is necessary to be aware of cultural traditions about gender and physical touch.

Voice Volume: In Yemeni communication, voice volume may also express messages. Although speaking loudly or aggressively may be perceived as confrontational or unfriendly, speaking softly and slowly is considered a gesture of respect and etiquette.

In Yemeni culture, personal space is a fundamental component of nonverbal communication. Yemenis typically chat while standing near one another, particularly when conversing with someone of the same gender.

Nonetheless, it's vital to observe cultural standards regarding physical contact and personal space when there are gender inequalities.

Generally, Yemeni society puts a lot of significance on nonverbal communication because it impacts how people interact and exchange meaning with one another.

3.4 The Importance of Language in Culture

Yemeni culture is heavily based on language, which has a considerable cultural effect.

The significance of language in Yemeni culture may be illustrated for the following key reasons:

Preservation of Heritage: Yemen's cultural past is considered to be maintained by the usage of language. Particularly Yemeni Arabic is viewed as a method of sustaining cultural continuity across generations and is a major component of the nation's identity.

Social Cohesion: Language is an important element for preserving social cohesion in Yemeni society. Yemeni Arabic is employed amongst many socioeconomic groups and is used as a medium of communication as well as a means of establishing togetherness and a sense of shared identity.

Expression of Identity: Both a person's and a society's identity may be communicated via language. One technique of stressing Yemeni identity and distinguishing it from other Arab states is the employment of Yemeni Arabic in particular.

Oral Tradition: Yemen has a rich tradition of oral history and storytelling, and language plays a key part in this culture. Language is vital to the oral tradition of cultural transmission that continues to be practiced by many Yemenis.

Religion: Islam is vital to Yemeni culture, and the Quran is written in Arabic. As a result, Yemen puts a high importance on the Arabic language from a religious and cultural standpoint.

Ultimately, language plays a crucial influence in Yemeni culture on a cultural, social, and religious level.

CHAPTER IV

Yemeni Cuisine & Customs

4.1 Traditional Yemeni Foods and Ingredients

The rich, aromatic cuisine of Yemen includes a variety of spices, herbs, and other ingredients.

The following are some traditional Yemeni meals and ingredients:

Saltah: A stew prepared with vegetables, meat, and a spice blend known as Hawayij, saltah is considered Yemen's national meal. It is commonly eaten with bread and served with a dollop of fenugreek paste.

Mandi: This well-known Yemeni dish is created by roasting meat in a tandoor oven—typically lamb or chicken—and then serving it over rice. Typically, black pepper, cumin, and coriander are used to season the meat.

Aseedah: A hearty Yemeni porridge frequently served with meat and vegetables that are created using wheat, water, and salt.

Bint Al-sahn: a Yemeni honey cake composed of layers of dough, honey, and butter that have been clarified. Sesame seeds are occasionally put on top.

Fahsa: A hot soup composed of vegetables, tomatoes, and shredded meat. It frequently comes with a side of hot sauce and bread.

Basbousa: Semolina, sugar, and rose water are mixed to form basbousa, a delicious cake that is sometimes topped with almonds or coconut.

Zurbian: A rice dinner with a variety of spices, tomatoes, onions, and meat (usually lamb or chicken).

Shakshouka: Served on bread, shakshouka is a dish cooked with tomatoes, peppers, onions, and eggs that are typically seasoned with cumin.

Fattah: A meal that comprises layers of bread, meat, yogurt, or tomato sauce. Toasted almonds are occasionally used as a garnish.

Thareed: a Yemeni delicacy that resembles bread pudding and is made by stacking bread, meat, and vegetables in a tomato-based broth.

Ma'akouda: A crispy-on-the-outside, soft-on-the-inside fried potato fritter that is typically served with a dipping sauce.

Bajela: Broad beans are cooked with spices, tomatoes, and garlic in a dish called bajela.

Lahoh: A bread that resembles a spongy pancake created from a batter of flour, water, and yeast.

Harisah: A dish made with cracked wheat and meat (typically lamb or chicken), which is cooked for hours until it takes on the consistency of porridge.

Fenugreek, cumin, coriander, cardamom, black pepper, turmeric, saffron, and dried limes are some prominent components in Yemeni food.

Dates, figs, pomegranates, okra, eggplant, and fava beans are just a few of the fruits, vegetables, and legumes utilized in Yemeni gastronomy.

Moreover, bread is a regular element in Yemeni meals, with types like khobz, malawah, and lahoh being popular options.

4.2 Traditions and Etiquette during Meals

In Yemen, dining together as a family is a regular and vital social event. When it comes to dining out, there are a few things to bear in mind.

Cleanse your hands before eating: This is a typical custom. In Yemen, washing your hands with a bowl and a small jug of water is traditional.

Eat with your right hand: As the left hand is typically used for personal hygiene, it is considered rude to eat with it. To scoop up the dish, pull a piece of bread off with your right hand.

Avoid wasting food: It is disrespectful in Yemeni culture to do so. It's vital to take only what you can ingest and to eat everything on your plate.

Take what you need: When helping yourself with a shared meal, only take what you need to reduce food wastage.

Refuse politely: Say "shukran, bas" (thank you, that's enough) to refuse graciously if you are offered more food than you can eat.

Share with others: It is normal to share food at the table, so make sure to do the same for those around you.

Respect the Host: Whenever you are a guest at someone's home, it is vital to treat them with respect. Never eat until being urged to do so by the host, and always express appreciation to them for the meal.

After everyone is done, don't get up from the table: To get up from the table before everyone has completed eating is considered impolite.

Say "bismillah" before starting your meal: It is usual to say "bismillah" before beginning your meal (in the name of God).

Drink tea after eating: Tea is typically drunk after meals to promote digestion and increase relaxation.

Overall, eating is an important social activity that has deep origins in Yemen's history and culture. You may respect and appreciate Yemeni culture and the persons who invite you to eat their meals by sticking to these customs and standards of civility.

4.3 Coffee and Qat Culture

Yemeni culture and social life are significantly impacted by coffee and qat, a plant whose chewed leaves have a stimulant effect.

Below is a description of Yemeni coffee and qat culture:

Coffee: While Yemen has a long history of coffee production and is famous for producing some of the finest coffee in the world, coffee is considered to have originated in Ethiopia. Coffee is typically served after meals to help digestion and stimulate discussion

Coffee is regularly offered in Yemen as part of a traditional rite called a "qahwa," which comprises roasting, grinding, and boiling the beverage in a special pot called a "dallah." Little cups are then filled with coffee and delivered with dates or other delicacies

Qat: When consumed, the leaves of the qat plant produce a mild stimulant. It is a mainstay of Yemeni civilization and is regularly consumed there. The effects of chewing qat, which generally continue for several hours, could be noticed in the late afternoon or evening

Chewing qat is a community habit that generally requires meeting with friends or family to speak about politics, the news, and other matters. Moreover, qat is employed in business and political events as an opener and relationship-building too

In Yemen, the production and consumption of qat are problematic because some people believe it contributes to economic instability and poverty, while others consider it a fundamental component of Yemeni culture and history

Overall, coffee and qat both have considerable cultural and social value in Yemen and are strongly rooted in the history and traditions of the country

4.3 Significance of Food in Yemen Society

Yemeni culture puts a great priority on food, and group meals are typically considered a method of establishing interpersonal bonds.

These are a few ways that food plays an important part in Yemen's culture:

Hospitality: Yemenis are recognized for their warmth and friendliness, and a large part of it is how they welcome people into their homes with food. Yemeni homes generally prepare huge, complicated dinners for guests, even if they are unwelcome one

Social Events: In Yemen, social events like weddings, religious festivals, and family reunions generally focus on food. These celebrations frequently entail big feasts with a broad assortment of traditional dishes

Cultural Identity: Yemeni food is rich and diversified, with various regional varieties and particular delights. Many Yemenis take delight in their regional cuisine and traditional meals as food is a vital component of their cultural identity

Nutrition: Fresh, healthful components including vegetables, grains, and legumes constitute the cornerstone of Yemeni cuisine. These foods are key to a balanced diet since they contain the necessary nutrition

Heritage and History: Yemeni cuisine has a strong heritage and a rich history that extends back thousands of years. Several Yemeni cuisines have been passed down through the years and play a key part in the culture of the country

Overall, food has a tremendous cultural effect on Yemen and is a fundamental element of daily life. From hospitality to social gatherings to cultural identity, food is a crucial component of what makes Yemeni culture unique and vibrant.

CHAPTER V

Arts and Culture

5.1 Traditional Yemeni Music and Dance

Yemeni dance and music are both rich and diverse, with a vast variety of traditions and styles.

The traditional music and dance of Yemen are characterized as follows:

Music: Ouds, a stringed instrument related to a lute, percussion instruments, and vocals are utilized regularly in Yemen music. The history and rich cultural heritage of Yemen affect the different locations' diverse musical traditions.

Sanaani, a well-liked type of Yemeni music, is a creation of the nation's capital Sana'a. The utilization of ouds, percussion instruments like the daf and mizmar, and call-and-response vocals distinguish this musical genre.

Other kinds of Yemeni music include "tihami," which originates from the Red Sea coast and includes powerful percussion beats, and "hadhrami," which is tied to the Hadhramaut region and employs the kamanja (a bowed string instrument).

Dance: Yemeni dance is diverse and varies depending on the area. Yemeni dances are commonly performed in groups and usually incorporate deft dancing and hand moves.

Men perform the traditional Yemeni dance "bar'a," which is recognized for its difficult maneuvers and acrobatics. "Lahji," another well-known Yemeni dance, is performed by females and is marked by elegant gestures and flowing clothes.

Yemenis also perform more current dances, such as the Middle Eastern line dance known as dabke, in addition to these old dances.

Overall, Yemeni music and dance play a key part in the nation's cultural heritage and are recognized for their capacity to transmit national identity and unite people in pleasure and celebration.

5.2 Visual & Applied Arts

Painting, calligraphy, embroidery, and pottery are just a few of the visual arts and crafts that Yemen has a long history of creating.

Following is a list of some of the most noteworthy visual arts and crafts made in Yemen:

Painting: Yemeni art has a long, distinguished history that dates back to antiquity. Bright colors and intricate patterns are typically employed by Yemeni painters, and ordinary life or religious themes are present in many of their pieces.

Calligraphy: Yemeni calligraphy is highly appreciated and commonly used to embellish books, buildings, and other artifacts. Yemeni calligraphers commonly incorporate verses from the Quran in their work and utilize several calligraphic styles, such as Kufic, Naskh, and Thuluth.

Embroidery: Yemeni embroidery is noted for its intricate designs and brilliant colors. Traditional Yemeni attire, such as the thobe, is typically adorned with needlework. Pillowcases and wall hangings are more examples of ornate home décor.

Pottery: Yemeni pottery is noted for its delicate shapes and intricate ornamentation. Yemeni potters generally utilize classic techniques like hand molding and wood burning, and many of their products feature complicated designs and vibrant colors.

Jewelry: Silver is widely used in Yemeni jewelry, which is recognized for its intricate designs and superb workmanship. Traditional Yemeni motifs like the hamsa (hand of Fatima), the moon, and the star are regularly used in the works of Yemeni jewelers.

Woodwork: Yemeni carvers are known for their precise carvings, which can be found on everything from doors and windows to furniture and decorative artifacts. Yemeni woodwork is characterized by its attention to detail and fine workmanship and generally contains geometric designs and floral motifs.

Textiles: Yemeni textiles are recognized for their intricate designs and brilliant colors. Natural fibers like cotton, wool, and silk are regularly utilized to make traditional

Yemeni textiles, which are then often ornamented using weaving, embroidery, and other techniques. Clothing, blankets, and decorative items are among the various things manufactured from Yemeni textiles.

Metalwork: Yemeni metalworkers are recognized for their exquisite workmanship and intricate designs. Yemeni metalwork is used to manufacture a variety of goods, including jewelry, lamps, and decorative objects. It commonly contains traditional motifs like the hamsa (hand of Fatima), the moon and star, and the tree of life.

Carpets: Yemeni carpets are recognized for their superb quality and complex designs. Natural fibers like wool and silk are typically utilized to manufacture Yemeni carpets, which are then adorned with traditional themes like floral and geometric designs. Yemeni carpets are regarded for their beauty and resilience and are used to decorate homes, mosques, and other buildings.

Generally, Yemeni visual arts and crafts are appreciated for their beauty, intricate patterns, and professional workmanship and constitute a vital component of the nation's cultural past.

The transfer of these skills from one generation to the next is vital for safeguarding Yemeni cultural traditions.

5.3 Literature & Poetry

Yemen has a rich history of poetry, oral storytelling, and written works, and it has a great literary tradition.

An overview of Yemeni poetry and literature is offered below:

Poetry: Yemeni poetry has a long and rich history, and it has produced some well-known poets over the years. Several

Yemeni poetry are known for their beauty and depth.

Poetry is commonly employed to express feelings and thoughts. Traditional Yemeni poetry is noted for its clever wordplay and use of metaphor, and it frequently follows precise rhyme and meter patterns.

Storytelling: Yemeni storytelling is a key component of the nation's cultural tradition. Many Yemeni legends are based on ancient myths and traditions, which are typically passed down orally from generation to generation. Moral precepts and delight may both be imparted via storytelling.

Written Works: Yemen has a strong legacy of generating literature, religious texts, and historical records in writing. There are some well-known works of Yemeni literature, including poetry, essays, and prose, that were written in classical Arabic.

Several works in Yemeni literature address subjects like social justice, morality, and spirituality, reflecting the nation's Islamic roots and cultural tradition.

Folk Literature: Yemeni folk literature encompasses several genres, including riddles, proverbs, and folktales. Folk literature is a key component of Yemen's cultural heritage as it typically represents the traditions and customs of numerous tribes and regions within the country.

Generally, Yemeni literature and poetry are appreciated for their beauty, depth, and cultural importance. They comprise an important component of the nation's cultural history.

These works are vital in sustaining Yemen's cultural identity as they portray Yemeni history and traditions.

5. 4 Recreation & Sports

Sport and leisure are firmly established in Yemeni culture, which has a rich cultural past. Sports and leisure have, however, been significantly harmed by the country's protracted conflict, with numerous facilities and events being suspended or destroyed.

Following are a handful of the most well-liked sports and leisure pastimes in Yemen:

Soccer: The most extensively played sport in Yemen is soccer. In regional events, such as the Gulf Cup and the Arab Cup, the national football team has had some success.

Camel Racing: Yemen has a long tradition of camel racing, especially in the countryside. The races commonly occur during festivals and other special events.

Wrestling: Another well-liked traditional pastime in Yemen, wrestling is commonly presented during festivities and rites.

Traditional Dance: The Al-Attab, Al-Sanaani, and Al-Shanfarah are three prominent traditional dances in Yemen.

Hunting: Hunting is a well-liked hobby in Yemen, especially in the countryside. The ibex, gazelle, and Arabian leopard are the most regularly employed game animals.

Basketball: Basketball is getting more and more popular in Yemen, especially among young people. The national basketball team has played in regional events since the Yemeni Basketball Federation was created in 1979.

Cricket: The Yemen Cricket Association was created in 1999, and cricket is also played there. The Asian Cricket Council Trophy was one of the regional events in which the national cricket team played.

Volleyball: Another well-liked sport in Yemen is volleyball, and the national volleyball team has played in regional games like the Asian Volleyball Championship.

Diving and Snorkeling: Yemen is a well-liked site for diving and snorkeling owing to its large coastline along the Red Sea and Arabian Sea. Yemen is regarded as having some of the largest coral reefs and marine life in the world.

Trekking & Hiking: The Arabian Peninsula's most stunning terrain, including mountains, valleys, and deserts, may be found in Yemen. In particular, in the Hadramaut Valley and the Haraz Mountains, hiking and trekking are well-liked sports.

It is crucial to underline that the continuous crisis in Yemen has had a severe effect on sports and leisure in the country, resulting in the interruption or destruction of various facilities and activities.

Participation in these activities has also been tough owing to a lack of resources and security. Yemenis continue to appreciate their cultural traditions and hope for a better future when leisure and sports can once again flourish.

CHAPTER VI

Yemen Holidays and Festivals

6.1 Islamic Observances & Holidays

Some of the prominent Islamic holidays and observances are mentioned below:

Eid al-Fitr: Ramadan, the Islamic holy month of fasting, finishes with this three-day festival. Muslims commemorate Eid al-Fitr by engaging in special prayers at mosques, giving gifts to loved ones, and preparing joyful feasts.

Eid al-Adha: The four-day celebration known as Eid al-Adha recalls the Prophet Abraham's (Abraham's) preparedness to give his son as a sacrifice to Allah. Muslims commemorate Eid al-Adha by engaging in special prayers at mosques, presenting a sacrificial animal—typically a sheep, goat, or cow—and donating the meat to the poor and impoverished.

Mawlid al-Nabi: On the 12th day of the Islamic month of Rabi al-Awwal, the Prophet Muhammad's birthday, known as Mawlid al-Nabi, is remembered. Muslims mark Mawlid al-Nabi by attending special mosque prayers, reading narratives of the Prophet Muhammad's life, and making special feasts.

Laylat al-Qadr: According to Muslims, this is the night during the final 10 days of Ramadan when the Prophet Muhammad purportedly heard the first verses of the Quran. On one of the holiest nights in the Islamic calendar, Muslims spend the night in prayer and reflection.

Ashura: This day of mourning remembers Imam Hussain, the grandson of the Prophet

Muhammad, who perished in the Battle of Karbala. It is observed by fasting, almsgiving, and mourning on the tenth day of the Islamic month of Muharram.

Ramadan: Muslims abstain from ingesting food, beverages, and other needs during the holy month of Ramadan, which lasts from sunrise until nightfall. It is a time for contemplation, more passionate prayer, and selfless gestures.

There are many more Islamic holidays and observances that Muslims over the world celebrate in addition to these notable ones.

This is because the Islamic lunar calendar is roughly 11 days shorter than the Gregorian calendar, it is crucial to note that the specific dates of many events and holidays may alter.

6.2 Holidays & Festivals at Home

The Islamic lunar calendar is utilized in Yemen to commemorate and celebrate religious holidays and observances.

In Yemen, the following prominent Islamic holidays and observances are observed:

National Day: Yemen's National Day is marked on May 22, the anniversary of the merger of North and South Yemen in 1990.

Isra and Mi'raj: This festival celebrates the Prophet Muhammad's ascension to heaven and his midnight journey from Mecca to Jerusalem. Muslims in Yemen engage in special prayers at mosques and hear narratives of the Prophet Muhammad's miraculous voyage to remember Isra and Mi'raj.

Day of Arafah: One of the holiest days in the Islamic calendar is the Day of Arafah, which comes the day before Eid al-Adha.

Muslims in Yemen spend the day in prayer and meditation, and it is stated that those who fast on this day will have their sins pardoned by Allah.

Laylat al-Bara'ah: According to Muslims, this night in the month of Sha'ban is a night of compassion and forgiveness. Muslims in Yemen spend the night in prayer and reflection, begging with Allah for their own and their loved ones' forgiveness.

Hadhrami Days: In the Hadhramaut region, the city of Mukalla conducts the celebration known as Hadhrami Days. It combines traditional music, dance, and food as it respects the area's rich cultural legacy.

Aden Summer Festival: Throughout the summer, the city of Aden holds this well-known event.

Yemeni Heritage Week: It is an annual festival that takes place in Sana'a, the country's capital. It incorporates exhibitions, lectures, and cultural performances to highlight Yemen's rich cultural legacy.

These are some additional Islamic feasts and festivals that are commemorated in Yemen. It is vital to remember that Yemen has a rich Islamic background, and the Yemeni people cherish their religious rituals and traditions in the greatest esteem.

6.3 Folklore and Holiday Customs

Yemen is a country with a diversified cultural heritage, which is reflected in its folklore and festival rituals.

These are a few instances:

Traditional Clothing: Yemeni men and women dress traditionally, according to the customs of their nation. The jambia, a curved dagger worn on a belt, is the most usual attire for guys. The dira'a, a clothing worn by ladies, is frequently highly colorful and embroidered.

Eating Qat: In Yemen, qat leaves are used as a stimulant. It is a social activity that pulls people together, and it typically goes along with chatting and exchanging tales.

Coffee: Coffee is an important component of Yemeni culture and is typically offered at social occasions. In the past, it was made in a miniature pot called a dallah and served in finjan, which are little cups.

Festivities Surrounding Weddings: Yemeni weddings are elaborate ceremonies that could stretch many days. They allow the family an opportunity to get together and celebrate by integrating traditional dances, music, and food.

Poetry: Poetry has a vital significance in Yemeni culture and is commonly recited in public places. It is a sort of storytelling and an outlet for emotion that is highly respected in Yemeni culture.

Festival of Al-Jidar: Sana'a, Yemen, celebrates the festival of Al-Jidar. The community has to join together and celebrate their culture which comprises painting houses in beautiful designs.

Festival of Al-Ramadi: Bayt al-Faqih is home to the celebration of Al-Ramadi. Men dressed in colorful traditional clothes and holding sticks conduct a traditional dance known as the al-Ramadi dance.

The Jumu'ah Prayer: The Friday prayer known as Al-Salat Al-Jumu'ah is done by Muslims throughout the world. It is an important social event in Yemen when people frequently dress to the nines and meet at the mosque for prayer and chat.

Festival of Al-Fasha: Taiz is the venue of the festival of Al-Fasha. It features traditional dances and music, as well as a parade of camels, horses, and other animals.

Al-Futuwwa: Al-Futuwwa is a traditional Yemeni philosophy that lays a significant focus on morality and ethical behavior. It comprises activities like self-discipline, altruism, and humility and is commonly associated with Sufi Islam.

Al-Mawlid: Al-Nabawi is a festival that Muslims all over the world celebrate to remember the birth of Prophet Muhammad. It is honored in Yemen with processions, Quran recitations, and the dissemination of sweets and other delights.

Al-Qaranqasho: On the fifteenth night of Ramadan, Yemen commemorates the event known as Al-Qaranqasho. Children dress up in costumes and knock on doors to collect candy and treats in this pastime.

Al-Hijri New Year: Also known as the Islamic New Year, Al-Hijri celebrates the Prophet Muhammad's journey from Mecca to Medina. It is marked with prayers, celebratory banquets, and gift-exchanging in Yemen.

Here are merely a few more examples of Yemen's folklore and festival rituals.

Every tradition plays a key part in the cultural inheritance of the country and develops a sense of connection and community among Yemenis.

CHAPTER VII

Yemeni Dress & Attire

7.1 Traditional Clothing and Styles

Yemen's regional distinctions in traditional clothing and fashion may be pretty noticeable.

Below are a few images of traditional Yemeni attire:

Men's Clothing: Yemeni guys often dress in a long, loose garment called a thawb. The thawb may be basic or embroidered, and it may be constructed of many materials like cotton, silk, or wool. Men also cover their heads with a kufiyyah, which is frequently tied with an agal, a headband that resembles a rope.

Women's Clothing: Yemeni females often dress in a long dress known as a dira'a. The dira'a is sometimes garlanded with sequins, beads, or needlework in brilliant hues. Women also cover their necks and hair with a headscarf known as a hijab.

Jambia: Many guys in Yemen carry the jambia, a traditional Yemeni dagger. It is commonly connected to a belt and may be adorned with valuable stones or intricate designs.

Makhila: A traditional Yemeni walking stick, the makhila is generally carried by males. It is sometimes adorned with silver or gold and is fashioned of juniper wood.

Al-Sirwal: Often worn by males in Yemen, al-sirwal is a form of traditional apparel. They are often loose-fitting and made of cotton or wool.

Al-Basht: Men typically wear the al-basht, a type of traditional cloak from Yemen. It is composed of wool and frequently contains cotton or silk lining.

Al-Ma'awiizah: Women in Yemen typically wear al-ma'awiizah, a form of traditional jewelry. It is generally constructed of silver and may be adorned with pearls or expensive stones.

Al-Mazwaji: Both men and women in Yemen wear this traditional form of dress. It consists of a long, flowing robe made of cotton or silk that is sometimes embroidered with exquisite features.

Al-Malaffah: Women typically wear al-Malaffah, a kind of traditional Yemeni dress. It consists of a long, flowing garment, often made of cotton or silk, that is embroidered with vibrant colors.

Al-Tarha: Al-Tarha is a form of traditional Yemeni headscarf that is worn by women. It is often crafted from cotton or silk and decorated with elaborate beading or embroidery.

Al-Dir'ah: Men wear al-Dir'ah, a form of traditional Yemeni attire. It is frequently constructed of cotton or silk and features a long shirt and loose-fitting pants.

Al-Sharshaf: Women commonly wear al-Sharshaf, a kind of traditional Yemeni dress. It consists of a long, flowing robe, commonly made of cotton or silk, that is embroidered artistically.

Al-Qutrah: Men commonly wear al-Qutrah, a form of traditional headpiece from Yemen. It consists of a tiny cap with a tassel that is commonly made of felt.

Al-Makhzani: Women usually wear al-Makhzani, a form of traditional Yemeni jewelry. It contains a set of bangles with magnificent designs that are frequently made of silver.

Here are only a few such examples of Yemeni traditional dress. Depending on the region and the occasion, Yemenis frequently dress in richly colored garments and accessories.

7.2 Islamic Dress and Modesty

Islam lays a significant focus on modesty, and Muslims are encouraged to dress in a specific manner. Here are some key details:

Hijab: Muslim women cover their hair, neck, and ears with the hijab, a headscarf. It is viewed as a display of humility and religious dedication. Depending on the culture and locality, the hijab may be worn in several ways and a vast range of styles, colors, and materials.

Modest Attire: Muslim women are recommended to wear modest attire, covering their full bodies from head to toe, in addition to the headscarf. Wearing loose-fitting garments that cover the arms, legs, and chest is the typical method. Muslim guys are also instructed to cover their bodies and wear modest attire.

Cultural Variations: Depending on the area and culture, Muslims may dress differently. For instance, women may opt to cover their complete body with a burqa or niqab in some countries while wearing a long garment and a headscarf in others.

Cultural Norms: In many Muslim countries, wearing traditional dress like long robes or kaftans is viewed as modest for both men and women. Modern dress is more common in various cultures, however, modesty is still prized.

Purpose of Modesty: Islam puts a great priority on modesty because it encourages respect, decency, and humility. It is moreover considered as a way of self-defense against unpleasant or unwelcome attention.

In general, modesty and clothing are key Islamic ideals, and Muslims are advised to dress in a way that preserves these beliefs.

While geographical and cultural variances may impact local dress regulations, the essential concepts of modesty and respect are universal.

7.3 Contemporary Fashion and Trends

Modern styles and popular fashion movements are referred to as contemporary fashion and trends. Many aspects, such as popular culture, social media, technology, and current events, affect these trends.

Oversized garments, monochromatic outfits, ecological and ethical fashion, genderless attire, and retro-inspired designs are just a few of the current fashion trends.

As shoppers become more mindful of how fast fashion impacts the environment and workers' rights, sustainable and ethical fashion has increased in popularity in recent years. Sustainable materials and production practices are increasingly being employed by businesses in their collections.

Unisex apparel that blurs the boundaries between traditional genders has also increased in favor. This fashion trend emphasizes diversity and inclusivity.

The resurrection of retro-inspired outfits from the 1970s, 1980s, and 1990s is another contemporary fashion trend. Trendy styles incorporate big shoes, huge coats, and high-waisted jeans.

Modern fashion and trends have been substantially affected by social media. Fashion influencers and corporations may now communicate with consumers and promote their creations on sites like Instagram and TikTok.

In general, current trends and fashion are always evolving and touched by a broad variety of aspects.

7.4 The Cultural Meaning of Clothing

The way we dress and what we wear has had a tremendous cultural effect throughout history and in many different nations. These are some examples of how clothing has cultural significance:

Cultural Identity: One's dress choices may serve as a manner of displaying their cultural identity and a sense of community. Traditional apparel, such as an Indian saree or a Japanese kimono, is commonly employed to portray cultural heritage.

Social Status: Clothing also may express social position, money, and power. Kings and nobility have worn costly and extravagant apparel throughout history to distinguish themselves apart from the average people.

Gender and Sexuality: Clothes are frequently used to express one's gender and sexual orientation. Dresses and skirts are related with femininity, while accessories like ties and suits are tied with masculinity.

Symbolism in terms of Religion: Clothes may have a religious connotation. For instance, religious leaders typically wear particular clothes to show their spiritual power. Dress modestly, which is praised in numerous religions like Islam and Judaism.

Historical Significance: Clothes may also indicate a given moment. For instance, flapper attire from the 1920s are typically used to represent the Roaring Twenties, a time of cultural revolution in the United States.

Regional Identity: Clothing may be used to express regional identity, particularly in countries with a range of cultural traditions. The qipao and cheongsam, two examples of traditional garments from diverse sections of China, may signify numerous cultural and historical influences.

Performance and Entertainment: Clothing may also be employed in entertainment and performance, such as in music, dancing, and theater. In addition to being used to transmit cultural and historical meanings, clothes and makeup are frequently applied to create a specific character or mood.

Political and Social Activism: Wearing garments with slogans or symbols that stand for a certain cause or movement is one way that clothing may be utilized to indicate political and social activism. For instance, the suffragette movement of the early 20th century adopted various colors to signify their cause, including purple, white, and green.

Globalization & Hybridization: As civilizations become more integrated and globalized, clothes may blend characteristics of different cultures. For instance, fashion designers might combine ethnic designs by combining traditional motifs or patterns from several cultures into their works.

Environmental Effect: Choosing clothing may symbolize one's principles and ideas regarding sustainability and ethical shopping. The apparel industry has a considerable environmental effect. It's a good idea to check with your insurance carrier to see if they give any discounts for the purchase of a prepaid card.

Generally speaking, clothing has a deep and diverse cultural significance that reflects both individual and community identities, histories, beliefs, and values.

CHAPTER VIII

Contemporary Issues & Challenges

8.1 Political and Economic Challenges

The following are some examples of the political and economic issues Yemen is today facing:

Conflict and Instability: The protracted conflict has led to instability and insecurity, which hurts millions of people's livelihoods and means of survival. Many individuals have been displaced as a consequence of the violence, which has also destroyed the infrastructure and interrupted economic operations.

Humanitarian Crisis: As a consequence of the war, there is a severe humanitarian crisis, in which millions of people require food, water, and medical assistance. The largest humanitarian calamity in the world, according to the UN, is in Yemen.

Economic Collapse: As a consequence of the conflict, the economy has collapsed, suffering from a dramatic decline in GDP, high inflation, and a shortage of foreign money. People now find it tough to acquire necessities as a consequence of the devaluation of the Yemeni rial and the subsequent drastic rise in price.

Trade and Investment Restrictions: This has been brought on by the conflict, which influences the accessibility and affordability of goods and services. Food and petroleum imports have been disrupted by the port blockade, resulting in shortages and price spikes.

Employment: With many enterprises failing and individuals being pushed to abandon their homes, the war has dramatically increased unemployment. The humanitarian situation has deteriorated as a consequence of the lack of economic opportunities.

Corruption: The economic situation in Yemen has gotten worse as a consequence of corruption and bad resource management. More individuals are suffering as a consequence of the support and resource misallocation that has hindered them from reaching those in need.

In conclusion, Yemen is suffering serious political and economic issues as a consequence of the extended wars and humanitarian crises.

The already terrible condition is being made considerably worse by the economy's collapse, trade and investment restrictions, excessive unemployment, and corruption, which makes it hard for people to access basics and creates widespread suffering.

8.2 Yemen's Humanitarian Catastrophe

Millions of people in Yemen are in dire need of humanitarian help as they deal with one of the largest humanitarian crises in history.

Yemen's persistent civil strife, the country's economic collapse, and constraints on humanitarian aid are all contributing causes to the country's humanitarian calamity.

Following are some key features of Yemen's humanitarian crisis:

Food Insecurity: As a consequence of the violence and the economic collapse, there is a significant food crisis, and millions of people are at danger of acute malnutrition.

According to estimates from the UN, 16.2 million people in Yemen lack access to food, and 50,000 are in famine-like situations.

Lack of access to Healthcare: Yemen's healthcare system has suffered tremendously from the conflict, with multiple hospitals and clinics being damaged or destroyed. The high fatality rate, particularly among minors, is a consequence of a shortage of medical supplies and skilled healthcare staff.

Scarcity of Water: It has created the development of water-borne infections like cholera—which has harmed millions of people in Yemen.

Displacement: Millions of people have been displaced as a consequence of the conflict, with many being driven to leave their homes and seek safety elsewhere. On top of their already poor access to necessities, this has put a significant weight on the host communities.

Child Protection: Children are particularly vulnerable in the conflict, with many fearing recruitment into armed groups, sexual exploitation, and abuse. In addition, child marriage and school dropout rates have considerably risen as a consequence of the conflict.

Limitations on Humanitarian Help: The violence has made it hard for those who give help to reach people who need it. The movement and access of humanitarian workers have been limited, and it has been difficult to import essential supplies like food and medicine owing to the blockade of ports.

In conclusion, millions of people in Yemen require urgent relief and the humanitarian tragedy is a multifaceted and diversified situation.

Some of the biggest challenges Yemenis confront include food insecurity, a lack of access to healthcare and clean water, relocation, child protection, and constraints on humanitarian support.

8.3 Gender Equality & Women's Rights

Gender equality and women's rights have been key concerns in many countries, including Yemen. Yemeni women experience various obstacles, including mobility and freedom limits, gender discrimination, and access to healthcare, education, and employment options.

The following are some key difficulties with women's rights and gender equality in Yemen:

Education: is not generally available to women in Yemen owing to many constraints. Few females attend primary school, and even fewer continue their education at the secondary and university levels. This hinders women's possibilities for social and economic growth.

Restriction on Movement: Women in Yemen are subject to limits on their freedom of movement and mobility. This limits their access to opportunities for employment, education, and healthcare. To travel or receive a passport, women must extra require authorization from a male guardian.

Discrimination in the Workplace: Women in Yemen have limited access to formal career opportunities and endure workplace discrimination. Women are underrepresented in leadership roles and often earn less money for doing the same job as men.

Early Marriage and Child Marriage: With many girls getting married off before the age of 18, Yemen has one of the highest rates of child marriage in the world. Early marriage inhibits girls' access to education and puts them at increased risk for maternal mortality, domestic violence, and other health difficulties.

Violence Against Women: Domestic abuse, sexual harassment, and rape are all widespread types of violence against women in Yemen. The frequency of gender-based violence has also escalated as a consequence of the conflict.

Restricted access to Healthcare: Yemeni women, particularly those who reside in rural locations, have restricted access to healthcare. This restricts their access to reproductive health care, which might have detrimental effects on their health.

In conclusion, women's rights and gender equality are important concerns in Yemen since they face obstacles to healthcare, work, and education as well as limitations on their freedom and movement.

For the sake of gender equality and the improvement of Yemeni women's lives, these issues must be addressed.

CHAPTER IX

Conclusion

9.1 Importance of Cultural Awareness in Yemen

Since it enables individuals to comprehend and respect Yemeni traditions, practices, and beliefs, cultural awareness is essential in Yemen.

Being culturally conscious is crucial to ensure that people accept and value the variety that exists in Yemen, a varied nation with a rich cultural legacy.

Following are some arguments for why cultural awareness is crucial in Yemen:

Increases Tolerance and Understanding: Being aware of one's cultural history could help one accept the differences that exist in Yemen. This knowledge increases tolerance and minimizes misinterpretations and arguments that might emerge from cultural differences.

Communicates Effectively: Yemeni culture has own language, customs, and traditions that may be distinct from those in other countries. People may communicate with Yemenis and comprehend their ideas more effectively by being culturally knowledgeable.

Building a Solid Connection: To have a solid connection with Yemenis involves cultural awareness, which creates respect and esteem for one another. Better economic possibilities, cross-cultural encounters, and friendships may arise from this.

Enhances Tourism: Yemen is a famous tourist destination owing to its rich cultural past. Travelers may enjoy and remember their trip better if they are culturally knowledgeable and can respect and appreciate the customs and traditions of the host nation.

Resolution of Conflicts: This is supported by cultural understanding, which is crucial for addressing any issues that might come from cultural disparities. People may find common ground and strive to settle conflicts by acknowledging and respecting one another's cultural values and opinions.

In Yemen, cultural awareness is vital because it encourages tolerance, respect, and understanding between persons from varied cultural origins. Also, it enhances relationships, increases communication, and assists in settling disagreements.

9.2 Advice on How to Interact with Yemeni Culture and People

Here are some recommendations to enhance your engagement with Yemeni culture and people:

Respect Regional Traditions: Yemen has a specific culture and a unique set of traditions that may not be identical to your own. Respect regional customs, including dress rules, social mores, and religious views.

Learn Basic Arabic: While many Yemenis speak English, learning a little Arabic may enhance your conversation and display your interest in their culture. Arabic is the official language of Yemen.

Be Patient and Respectful: Take your time when chatting with Yemenis as they value patience and politeness. While conversing with them, be courteous, patient, and respectful.

Participate in Cultural Events: Yemen has a rich cultural past and visiting events like music festivals and dance performances may help you understand and appreciate Yemeni culture better.

Avoid complex problems: A complex political and social climate exists in Yemen, making some problems sensitive or controversial. Politics, religion, and other difficult matters should not be mentioned unless your Yemeni counterparts bring them up.

Demonstrate Interest in Yemeni cuisine: Yemeni cuisine is delicious and diverse, so take an interest in it and taste some of the regional specialities. This will convey that you appreciate their customs and culture.

Be Open: Be open to learning about Yemeni culture and customs. You may create deep ties and cross-cultural understanding by doing this.

Handshake to greet: Yemenis typically shake hands to greet one another, hence it is proper to do the same. Be cautioned, therefore, that some traditional Yemenis may prefer to greet people of the same gender.

Dress Modestly: Respect the traditional culture of Yemen by wearing modestly, especially when visiting places of worship. Men should avoid from sporting shorts or sleeveless shirts, while ladies should cover their hair and wear loose-fitting clothing that covers their arms and legs.

Demonstrate Interest in Family and Community: Yemeni culture puts a great priority on family and community, hence expressing an interest in the health of someone's family or community may be a good strategy to creating relationships.

Bring Presents: Yemenis commonly offer presents, so bringing something simple like flowers or candy could be a lovely way to convey your thanks and promote friendship.

Be Conscious of Gender Roles: Remember that gender roles are more clearly defined in Yemen than in many Western nations as it is a patriarchal society. Be cognizant of these gender conventions and treat them with respect, especially when speaking to someone of the opposing sex.

Active Listening: It is vital when chatting with Yemenis about their culture and people. Spend some time listening to what others have to say, and then convey your interest in their opinion by asking questions.

Be Mindful of Social norms: Yemeni culture has its own set of social norms that may not fit with your own. Be conscious of these social etiquette norms, such as when it's nice to visit someone's home or how to eat with your hands.

In conclusion, connection with Yemeni culture and people involves a friendly and responsive approach.

You may create healthy relationships and increase cultural understanding by shaking hands, dressing modestly, displaying interest in family and community, delivering gifts, being sensitive of gender roles, actively listening, and being careful of social procedure.

Made in the USA
Middletown, DE
01 November 2024

63711598R00064